Note to Parents and Teachers

The READING ABOUT: STARTERS series introduces key science vocabulary to young children while encouraging them to discover and understand the world around them. The series works as a set of graded readers in three levels.

LEVEL 1: BEGINNING TO READ follows guidelines set out in the National Curriculum for Year 1. These books can be read alone or as part of guided or group reading. Each book has three sections:

• Information pages that introduce new words. These key words appear in bold throughout the book for easy recognition.
• A lively story that recalls this vocabulary and encourages children to use these words when they talk and write.
• A quiz and word search ask children to look back and recall what they have read.

THINGS THAT GO looks at MOVEMENT. Below are some activities related to the questions on the information spreads that parents, carers and teachers can use to discuss and develop further ideas and concepts:

p. 5 *Can you move parts of your body fast and slow?* Could extend this in a PE class by asking children to change speed of movement and the way they make movements.

p. 7 *Can you walk sideways like a crab, or backwards?* Exploring basic movements, using animal examples, e.g. snake, kangaroo, bird. In a clear, safe space children could also copy simple movements made by a teacher, playing the game "Simon says".

p. 9 *How do you make a bicycle turn around a corner?* You could extend this by talking about how different vehicles turn and how they are steered, e.g. car, boat, plane.

p. 11 *What parts of their body do animals climb with?* E.g. cats/bears with claws, monkeys with grasping tails, snails with sticky, muscular foot.

p. 13 *Can you walk in water? What can't you do?* Movement in water, e.g. swimming. Could extend by talking about floating/sinking and safety issues concerning water.

p. 15 *What shapes can you make with your body?* Allow children to try out and practise their ideas, using stimuli such as words, poetry, pictures, sounds and objects.

p. 19 *What else do you push and pull?* Think about bigger movements such as hitting ball/pushing a swing/tug-of-war and smaller movements such as typing/playing an instrument. Children could also mime different actions.

p. 21 *How can you cross a road safely?* Could extend by talking about other potentially dangerous machines/objects, e.g. lawnmowers, electrical appliances, sharp tools.

ADVISORY TEAM

Educational Consultant
Andrea Bright – Science Co-ordinator, Trafalgar Junior School, Twickenham

Literacy Consultant
Jackie Holderness – former Senior Lecturer in Primary Education, Westminster Institute, Oxford Brookes University

Series Consultants
Anne Fussell – Early Years Teacher and University Tutor, Westminster College, Oxford Brookes University

David Fussell – C.Chem., FRSC

CONTENTS

© Aladdin Books Ltd 2004

Designed and produced by
Aladdin Books Ltd
2/3 Fitzroy Mews
London W1T 6DF

First published in
Great Britain in 2004 by
Franklin Watts
96 Leonard Street
London EC2A 4XD

A catalogue record for this
book is available from the
British Library.

ISBN 0 7496 5593 3

Printed in UAE

All rights reserved

Editor: Sally Hewitt

Design: PBD; Flick, Book
Design and Graphics

Picture research:
Brian Hunter Smart

Thanks to:
• The pupils of Trafalgar Infants
School, Twickenham for
appearing as models in this book.
• Lynne Thompson for helping
to organise the photoshoots.
• The pupils and teachers of
Trafalgar Junior School,
Twickenham and St. Nicholas
C.E. Infant School, Wallingford,
for testing the sample books.

Photocredits
*Abbreviations: l-left, r-right, b-bottom,
t-top, c-centre, m-middle*
Front cover tl, 25mr — Corbis Royalty
Free. Front cover tc, 11r, 23c — Jim
Pipe. Front cover tr, 2bl, 6mr, 7 both,
9 both, 12br, 13t, 16b, 22b, 29tl, 31tr,
32tr, 32mrt — Digital Stock. Front
cover b, 2ml, 10bl, 18b, 32ml 32bl,
32mrb — Comstock. 2tl, 15tr, 24t,
25bl, 30ml — Digital Vision. 3t, 19br,
20mr, 22t, 29br, 32br — Photodisc. 3b
, 4t, 8tl, 10tr, 14br, 15bl, 15bm, 15br,
17 both, 19t, 26 both, 28 both, 31ml —
PBD. 5tr — Otto Rogge Photography.
5b — Chris Desmond/U.S. Navy. 6tl,
8mr, 11tl, 18mr, 20tl, 21, 31bl, 32tl,
32mlt — Corbis. 12t, 14t, 30tr, 32mlb,
32mr — Brand X Pictures. 13b —
Rebecca J. Moat/U.S. Navy. 16t, 27tr,
31mr — Flat Earth. 23tr — Yamaha.
24br, 25tl, 25tr, 27bl — Corel.

MOVEMENT

Things that Go

by Jim Pipe

Aladdin/Watts

London • Sydney

It is fun to **move** your body.
It feels good too!

When you **walk**, you go **slow**.
When you **run**, you go **fast**.

4

Machines and animals **move** too.
Some things are **slow**. A snail **moves**
very **slowly**.

Some things
move fast.
A racing car
is very **fast**.

• Can you move parts of your body fast and slow?

What makes you move?

You walk and run with your legs.

You **swing** from bars with your arms.

You **crawl** on your hands and knees.

To **swing** backwards and forwards, you move your arms and legs.

You can move in water too. You move your arms and legs to **swim**.

• Can you walk sideways like a crab, or backwards?

You **turn around**
a corner.
You **turn** left or right.

If you look **around**,
you **turn** your head.

8

If you **turn** when you are going fast, you **swerve**.

Your body leans over.

This motorbike is **swerving around** a corner.

• How do you make a bicycle turn around a corner?

How can you move upwards?

You can **hop** up and down on one leg.

This dog **jumps** up into the air.

If you **jump** up, do you come down?

10

You **climb** upwards too.
You **climb** up and down the stairs.

You can **climb** with your arms and legs.

• What parts of their body do animals climb with?

How can you
move downwards?
You can **slide**
down a **slide**.

If the ground is wet and **slippery,**
you can **slip** over. Whoops!

12

You can **dive** down into water. Splash!

You can **dive** under the water too.
A submarine **dives** down deep.

• Can you walk in water? What can't you do?

A wheel **spins**
round and round.

If you **twist** a lid,
it **spins** round too.

Round objects **roll**.

A wheel **rolls**
along the ground.
A ball **rolls** too.

Can you **roll** like a ball or a wheel?
Can you **spin** or **twist** your body?

Twist   **Roll**   **Cartwheel**

• What shapes can you make with your body?

When things **stop**, they do not move.

A train **stops** at the station.

It stands **still**.

When the train **starts**, it moves again.

Before a race, you all stand **still**.
When it **starts**, you all move.
At the end, you all **stop**!

• What other things start and stop?

Pushes and **pulls** make things move.
You **push** and **pull** a friend's cart.

When you throw
a ball, you **push** it.
A kick is a **push** too.

A **push** makes a roundabout spin.
A **push** or **pull** makes it spin **faster**.

A **pull** can make things **slower** too. Hang onto a friend and see!

• What else do you push and pull?

The **wind** makes things move.
When it **blows**, flags flap and flutter.

The **wind blows** a sail boat along on
the water. It makes **waves**.

Water makes things move too.

A **wave** can push you over.
A big **wave** can pull you under.
So be careful in the sea!

• What else moves when the wind blows?

Your body makes you move.
Engines make **machines** move.
Engines push planes into the sky.
They help them to **fly**.

Engines push ships through the water.

Engines push cars and motorbikes along the road.

Where is the **engine** on this motorbike?

Cars and trucks are heavy **machines**.
They can squash you.
So be careful near roads!

• How can you cross a road safely?

I want to go to the park.
"Oh no!" says Dad, "Not again!"

I love the park.
There is lots to do.
My friends love
the park, too.

You can ride a
bike at the park.

You can **swim** and **dive**
in the lake.

You can **fly** a kite.
The **wind blows** a
kite into the sky.

I **climb** onto Dad.
Dad is too **slow**.
"**Faster**, Dad! **Run!**" I say.

"Oh no!" says Dad.

All my friends are at the playground.

We **climb** on the bars.
We **slide** down the **slide**.

Raj and Mary **hop**
across the steps.

"Oh no!" says Dad,
"They might **slip!**"

Susie and I go
on the seesaw.

We **push** hard
and it **moves**
up and down.

We go on the
swings. I give
Lucy a big **push**.

"Oh no!" says
Dad, "Lucy
might **fly** off!"

Sara **climbs** up the **slide.** Whoosh! She **slides** down **fast.**

We **jump** on the roundabout. It **spins round** and **round.**

We **push** and the roundabout **spins faster.**

"Oh no!" says Dad.

Tom **starts** off on his bike. Katie **pulls** on her skates.

Katie **turns** left and right. She **swerves around** a corner.

Tom **rolls** down a hill. He goes **faster** and **faster**.

"Oh no!" shouts Dad. "**Stop!** You will **roll** into the lake!"

Phew! Tom **stops** and **turns** his bike **around**. While Dad watches Tom, we get the hose.

We spray water at Dad. Now he **runs fast!**

"Oh no!" I laugh. "You might get wet!"

Write down words about movement:
- **jump** • **dive**
- **roll** • **hop** • **slide**

Make the words do what they say!

QUIZ

How do you **crawl?**

Answer on page 6

How do you **move** a lid?

Answer on page 14

Where does a train **stop?**

Answer on page 16

What **blows** a sail boat along?

Answer on page 20

Did you know the answers? Give yourself a

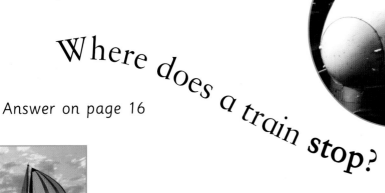

Do you remember these **movement** words?
Well done! Can you remember any more?

 **swing**
page 6

swim
page 7

 **turn**
page 8

swerve
page 9

 **jump**
page 10

slide
page 12

 **spin**
page 14

push
page 18

 **pull**
page 18

fly
page 22